Dedication

To everyone who wants to be financially free

TRANSCEND OR DIE TRYING

PROJECT SELF - TRANSCENDENCE

Table of Contents

Section 1:

What is Online Business?

Introduction

Online business refers to a business that is started on the Internet. As you know, the internet is a vast place and helps in connecting the world from corner to corner. You can make use of it to start and operate your business. This activity can range from freelancing to retail therapy and also blogs.

There is a lot of ways to make money online. You don't really have to be an internet expert to create an online business. Many people wonder if it will be possible for them to quit their day job and take up online business full time. From my experience, it's totally possible. It's possible for you to take it up full time provided you dedicate yourself to it. I'm not saying it'll be easy.

Can anybody start making money online?

Anybody interested in taking up online businesses can take it up. There is no age limit, and as long as you have the time and skill for it, you can start an online business. You don't have to spend too much money to start with it and will only require a working laptop and internet connection.

Will I be able to earn a good living?

How much you earn depends on how skilled and efficient you are. Many people have made a living be starting online businesses. I'm one of them; you also can do the same if you are dedicated enough and take it up seriously. Even if it is a bit slow in the beginning, you must not lose patience and continue with it. With time, you will see that your business has grown by leaps and bounds, and you can draw in quite a handsome sum on a monthly basis.

Is this a long-term solution?

Online businesses are sustainable. You can continue with it for as long as you like. There is no time frame or expiry date. It depends on how serious you are about it and how long you want it to last. Once you start, there is no need for you to terminate your business and can continue with it for as long as you like.

Can I do this part-time?

From my experience, if you wish to remain with your full-time job and take the online business up as a part time job, then that is possible. But you will need to find a good virtual assistant and use more freelancer in order to do everything efficiently. Remember; your emotional energy is limited. You cannot do everything by yourself.

My belief is simple - we humans can achieve anything we want unless we want with our whole being.

Chapter 1:

How To Set Up Your Online Business

Choose Your Niche

In my opinion, the first thing to do is select the area in which you wish to start your online business. It's probably the most important step, and you have to choose the best business to start. Through the course of this book, we will look at the different options that you have regarding online money-making activities. You must go through each of them in detail and understand their individual pros and cons before deciding on one of them. If you already have an idea of what you want to do, then you can follow the following steps one by one.

First things first - Market research

The next step is to perform a market research. You have to understand who your target audience is and how you can appeal to them. Maybe the market does not need your product or service. Just search for others who are making money with it. If the answers is yes, that means the market is profitable.

Product/Service Development

The next step is to develop the product or service that you wish to market. Whether it is a consumer product or a consumer service, you have to develop it to the best of your ability. If you already have a product, then you must see if it is salable on a large scale or you need to make modifications to it. The ultimate goal is to reach out to as many people as possible and increase the size of your business. If you're starting from scratch, then you might have to come up with the product or service and do a test run to see if it is a good product. I will do deeper into product development later in the book.

Preparation

The next step is to make necessary preparations. For example, if you would like to open a blog site then choose something like Wordpress to host it. If you want to start making videos – download video editing software and master it. If you can't do it yourself - find someone who can. It requires you to do research on what you need.

Domain and Website

You must create a website and decide on a domain name. You have to design the site in such a way that it is apt for your business. You can make use of a preset template for the website or create something from scratch. The latter is a better choice as compared to the former as you will have the chance to customize the site to your liking. If you have a blog and wish to create a website, then you can transfer the data. Once your site is up, you must test it out and ensure that everything is working well. For example, if you want to start selling books on Amazon – set up your Amazon Author webpage.

Your Competition

The next step in the process is looking at your competition and seeing what they are offering to their customers. You must look at their websites and products and services. But don't copy anything from them. You should only see it see how they are presenting themselves to their customers and the types of products and services that they are offering.

Promote and Advertise Your Business

The next step is to advertise your business and let everybody know about it. The best way to do is by making use of your social media. Add links to your website everywhere and encourage more and more people to visit it. You will see that hordes of people have visited your site and that social media is helping you in a big way. You can also get others to advertise for you and mention about you in their blogs and social media platforms. **In my opinion**, you will get the most traffic from social media. You can add latest pictures of all your products and services. You have to keep updating the pages from time to time. Link all your accounts and ensure that people know you are the same company. You must employ someone to look at the reports on a daily basis and have interactive sessions with your customers. You have to use the platform to your advantage and make the most of it. One of the best ways to promote yourself is to use "Facebook Dark Posts". Search it now!

Build Your Client Base

Once everything is done, you have to rely on your customer or client base. It's probably the most important step in the process. It is not enough to have customers, and you need to build on it and increase the number. The best way to do so is by asking your current customers to recommend you to others that they know. If you're a freelancer and need more clients, then you should ask your current clients to refer to others and so on. *My mentality - you should never be satisfied with what you have. Always push FORWARD. Another great way is to build an email list.*

Motivation: Your Vision

It is important for any company to prepare a vision and mission statement. The vision statement should speak what your business stands for and where you wish to see yourself in a few years' time The mission statement, on the other hand, should signify what you want to attain through your company. Once you have defined it, you must have it printed and placed in your home office to remain motivated.

Motivation: Goals

Write down your goals. These can be weekly, monthly or yearly objectives and should remind you of what you are after. Everybody works towards individual goals in their business, and once you have them predefined, you will be able to work towards them. Remember to write down reasonable goals that are attainable. Maintain a list of the goals handy and as soon as they are attained, tick them off of the list. Your goal list will help you remain motivated and continue with your business.

Plan all Your Finances

Raising funds is the next step. If you're looking to start a website, then you will have to set aside a little money to pay towards the web host on a monthly basis. If you plan to be a freelancer then you have to plan on the finances that will be required to pay for any software and Internet connections, you have to think about the payment needed for the logistics for your online store, etc. Similarly, you have to plan all your finances in advance and remain prepared for your business.

Your Office/Location

The next step is to decide on the place. If you wish to work from your home, then you should choose a place to set up a home office. You have to have a dedicated space. If you wish to sell physical products, then you should choose a warehouse to put all your additional products where they will stay until they are ready to be shipped. Find a good shipping company; outsourcing is key here.

Making money as Freelancer

When I started working online, my funds were limited. Thankfully, I began working as a freelancer and all money I earned working for other people online – I invested in building my Amazon product selling business. Now my manager manages my freelancing accounts and does all the orders for me. It may be hard at the beginning, but the more reviews you get, the easier it gets.

Writing and Editing

It's probably the most widely chosen form of freelancing. As a freelance writer, you will have to find clients to write for. These customers can be individuals or companies. If you wish to contribute to an online newspaper, then you will have to scour for opportunities. Leading news sites encourage freelance articles that they will publish from time to time. You can also approach online magazines for the same. If you're looking for something more dependable, then you can check out websites like Upwork and Freelancer, where many people would have advertised their need for a writer. You can choose a topic of your interest and approach them for the job. If they like your work, you will be awarded. Apart from articles, you will also have the choice to write eBooks. If you don't want to work for someone, then you can write your book and publish it on Amazon.

Every time someone buys your book, you will get paid for it. You can also offer your services as the freelance writer on sites such as Fiverr, where you will find clients that are looking to award jobs to freelancers for $5. There is no limit to how many clients you can have and the more you have, the better as you will have a consistent supply of work.

If your expertise lies in editing, then you can find stuff to edit as well. Again, you can look for an online job where you get to write articles. There is no limit on the number of clients that you can have. You can make use of your existing work to find new work by supplying samples.

Mentoring others

You can become an online teacher if you like. You can look for websites that require teachers or instructors for individual subjects. You live in any part of the world, as long as you have a computer, with an internet connection. You must also solve their issues and assign them homework. You can have as many students as you like and there is no limit on the subjects that you can pick. Great website to publish your own course is Udemy.

Showing Your Language skills – Translations

You can become a translator for online websites and also eBooks. You will have to look for clients that are interested in having their material translated into a language that you are familiar with. As long as you know to translate the words and sentences, you can take up the job. Here too, there is no limit to the amount of work that you can take up. You can work on multiple projects at the same time depending on your translating skills. If you know a lot of languages then it will only work in your favor.

Photography and Image Editing

There is a lot of demand for photography these days, as all websites require quality photos. If you are skilled at taking good pictures then you can take up freelance photography jobs. All you're required to do is look for a client and get an assignment. When you understand the specifications, you take quality photos and submit them. After approval, you will be paid for it. Remember; you will need a good quality camera and the skill to take good pictures. To get more clients, you can start a photography blog and add in all the best images that you have taken. Don't forget to watermark it, as there is scope for photography theft online. You will get paid for it every time someone orders the products with your photos printed on it.

Music and Composing

If you know to play an instrument or can sing then you can offer those services. Clients will need jingles or a song that you will have to compose for them. They will provide you with the guidelines, and you are required to remain within the confines and write music. You can also create a course on any music instrument you have mastered. Possibilities are limitless.

Chapter 2:

How To Sell Products Online

If you plan to get into retail or consumer business online then you will have to take another approach. Here I tell you how to open an online store. Before we look at it in detail, you have to understand that there are two ways to go about it. The first way is to tie up with an existing retailer like Amazon or eBay, and the other way is to have a website of your own. In my opinion, this is the best way to make money online, creating an online shop is like building a real business. It is not a get rich quick thing; it requires times and patience.

Amazon

The first way is to become a seller on Amazon or eBay. There are a few steps that you must follow, and they are as follows.

• First, decide what you wish to sell. Once you have decided, you must acquire several pieces of it. That you can do by ordering it in bulk from a site like Alibaba.com or Aliexpress.com. Both of these will allow you to get in touch with bulk sellers based out of China. Once you identify the vendor, you can ask for samples. If you like the samples, then you can order it in bulk.

• Then, create a profile on Amazon and fill in all the details. You have to provide all the correct information.

• Once your profile is created, you should list the items that you wish to sell. You have to describe the products in the best way and mention its features.

• Try to upload the latest pictures of the product and one shot from every angle. You have to use a high-quality camera to take the pictures or can also use the same images that have been supplied by your wholesaler.

• You would have noticed that some sellers will appear as the first and recommended sellers and the others will be bunched into a list. You have to strive to be the first and the recommended seller if you wish to experience elevated sales.

• You have to try and maintain an excellent image, and the best way to do so is by getting as many positive reviews for your company and products as possible.

• As soon as somebody orders your product, Amazon will notify you, and you should pack and dispatch it. Amazon also gives you the option to send your products in bulk to their go down, and they will do the dispatching themselves.

• It is also a good place to sell items from your personal collection such as dolls and antique pieces. Best place to sell things like that is ebay.

• Once your store starts to roll, you can expand and sell many other products as well.

• When you launch the business, you have to ensure that your company's name is unique and not something that already exists.

• You have to have little patience with your enterprise and have reasonable expectations. You cannot expect to become the best seller overnight and have to wait a while before you can make it big.

Shopify

• If you wish to sell the products on your website then here are the steps to follow.

• The first step is to choose the products that you want to sell. If you already are a seller, then you can move to the third phase.

• Contact someone from Alibaba.com and buy the products in bulk.

• Next, you have to write down a business plan. You have to decide the logistics, the warehouse, employees, taxes, etc.

• Now create a website for yourself which will serve as an online store.

• You will have to make use of specific software that helps in creating online stores. It will provide you with appropriate options that are part of online stores.

• You have to choose a host for your website and ensure that you pick a good one. Shopify is widely used by many sellers; I also use Shopify, because it's very easy to use.

• Once your site goes live, you can customize it and add in all the features. If you don't know how to do it then, you can avail the help of a website designer.

• You will also have to create an about page, a home page, product description pages etc.

• Don't forget to register your company.

• Next, tie up with e-commerce software like PayPal, as you have to get paid for the products that you sell.

• Once everything is created, you must visit the website to see if everything is proper.

• You should also get others to check it out for you.

• Once the site is up, you should spread the news about it.

• Use social media to promote your page.

• You also have to make use of SEO to be found on the internet.

• You have to establish contact with as many people as possible if you wish to make your online business success.

These are the different steps that you must adopt when you want to start an online store. You can always hire a mentor, find an online course that will help you to all the small tasks and optimize your business.

Chapter 3:

Blogging and Affiliate Marketing

The very first thing to do is pick the topic for the blog. You will have a lot of subjects to choose from, and you must select the one that is the best. Choose interesting topics that are trending currently and write information that people will not find anywhere else.

There is no point in supplying information that is already present on the web. Once you pick the topics, you must do a thorough research on the subject and write informative and exciting articles. I personally know a few guys who make over 5000$ a month with affiliate marketing. If they can do it, everyone can do it. *Everything requires time and effort.* Some themes for your future blog:

Technical and Electronics

These are one of the most popular topics that people write on. Right from knowledge on computers to apps, people need information to operate their devices. They will turn to blogs and websites that provide people with comprehensive information on the topic. You can pick a topic and write extensively on it.

Fashion Blog

Fashion is the next most popular topic that gets discussed on the internet. Right from the latest fashions to shoes and accessories, there is a lot of demand for the information. You can recommend new styles, write about new brands, other fashion products, etc.

Alternate sciences

Topics such as tarot predictions, numerology, and Feng Shui are all interesting subjects. You will have a lot of takers for it. You can write extensively on these themes are they are easy, and you will find a lot of information on it. All you have to do is look for a new topic to focus on each time and write extensively.

Creating money online

These blogs are very popular because people want to make money. Most people wish to make a lot of cash, and you could help them to achieve it. If you've already started making money online, it will give you much more credibility. Create an online course, write an Ebook and sell it to your audience!

Another topics could be something like: gaming, health related, spirituality, travelling, social skills

Chapter 4:

How To Market on Social Media - SEO

Facebook Marketing

As I mentioned, Facebook is the best way to promote your business. Every morning, millions of users login to interact with others on this platform. I'm sure you too have an account and many friends in your list. You have to make use of this situation and allow Facebook to do your business good. Start by creating a Page for your company. You must fill in all the appropriate details and then invite everybody in your list to like the page. You can then use this page to advertise your products and services. You can employ someone to update your page from time to time. Ensure that you make use of all the latest pictures of your products. You must announce contests and publish exciting news on your page to keep your customers' interest up.

Twitter Marketing

Twitter is the next best social media platform that you can use for your online promotions. Twitter allows you to share your products' information and can also add in 140 character taglines. You can reach millions of people worldwide, and it is extremely easy for you to maintain the account. You have to know to use hashtags and @ and direct the campaign at specific target groups. You can also start a revolution with the hashtag trend and pick on a viral topic. You can add links from your Instagram account to share photos and videos on your Twitter account. You can also host live podcasts to interact with your customers.

Instagram Marketing

Instagram is a photo-sharing site that you can use to reach your customers. You can share pictures of your products and can make it interactive. You must take high-resolution photos and post it. It also pays to post interesting pictures of people using your products. You can capitalize on the power of your fans and repost their images. If you have influential friends like celebrities, then you can ask them to repost your photos and make your brand popular. It is possible for you to embed the links to your Instagram pictures in your blog and also other social media platforms. Another great way to promote your product is to create Instagram page and put photos related to your product or service and use hashtags.

Chapter 5:

Most Common Mistakes and Why You Should Avoid Them

Start on the Right Foot

Many people get over enthusiastic and start wrong. They will not have a clear idea of the task ahead and jump into it. If you do so, then everything will come undone. My friend, you have to remain patient and start on the right foot. Take your time conduct appropriate research on the topic. You can also employ a mentor if you like. Ask him or her questions and clear all your doubts. It also pays to have a role model that you can emulate. Once you are confident, you can start with the business.

Hesitating way too long

Once you have everything ready, don't wait too long to launch your business. You will surely have apprehensions when you wish to start a business but waiting on it for too long will prove to be a mistake. If you are developing a product or service, then try to do it fast. Set a deadline for yourself and attempt to meet it. You will see that being on time greatly helps in getting the work done more quickly and in an efficient manner. While the product is being prepared, you can start with the process of creating the website.

Not Thinking about Your Customers

It is paramount to remain in the good relationships with your customers and clients. Don't make the mistake of ignoring their input and try to stay as friendly and interactive with them as possible. Many companies talk with their customers to understand them better. You must start following them on social media sites and follow their every move. That mainly applies to your regular customers. You have to send those emails and messages regularly. It pays to employ a social media expert to help you with the job. You can also ignore this step, but if you want to create a long-term business, you shouldn't avoid this.

Lack of Workplace

Don't make the mistake of not having an office at home. You cannot work on your couch and have the television on in front of you. You will end up making mistakes or remain distracted. Ensure that you set up a home office and have a dedicated computer system in place. Decide upon an appropriate timing and ensure that you begin work at the same time daily.

Lack of Seriousness

Don't be too casual about your job. You must not encourage your family members disturbing you during office hours. They should understand how dangerous your work is and not bother you. You must ideally lock yourself in your room and step out only after your job is done. It pays to make use of a Do Not Disturb sign to tell them how serious you are about your job. It will also pay to dress up like you are going to the office.

Getting Discouraged by Negativity

Do not get bogged down by negative feedback. There will always be someone who will try to bring you down. They might say nasty things about your company or products on social media platforms, but you must not take it to heart. If there is constructive criticism then work on it but don't get unnecessarily disturbed by comments that random people make.

Chapter 6:

Summary

As you know, the Internet is a vast place, and there are millions of users. You can capitalize on this aspect and earn an income by starting a business. There are many ways in which you can start a business online. All you need is an internet connection, and you are ready to make some cash. It is very easy to begin, provided you know how to go about it in a step-by-step manner. The very first thing to do is to acquire as much knowledge on the subject as possible. This book will provide you a lot of essential information on the subject, no doubt, but you must not limit yourself to just that. You have to turn to other sources as well and increase your knowledge to the highest possible extent. At the end of the book, I will provide you with valuable resources, other guys who inspire me. Once you start with it, you will see how easy it is to continue on and will be motivated to take it from strength to strength.

There are many advantages to starting an online business. The uses differ from person to person but there are a few primary reasons that make online business the most sought after form of business ventures. Firstly, it gives the person freedom to work from anywhere and not have to commute to the office. Some people work from beaches and still make a lot of money through their online business ventures. Another advantage is that you will not have an annoying boss breathing down your neck. You will have the freedom to be your boss and decide how much work you want to do. There is also the advantage of earning while you're studying and make good money. I'm a student myself, and I'm euphoric that I started my own thing.

There are many types of online businesses to choose from. You can sell items online by tying up with Amazon or eBay. You can also start an online store and sell products or services. There is no limit to what you can sell and right from clothes to jewelry to cakes, the options are unlimited.

You must make use of social media to the highest possible extent. We saw how you can use Facebook, Twitter, Instagram to your advantage and must capitalize on their power to improve you're the scope of your online business.

Having reasonable expectations out of your company is crucial. Time is a big factor, and you need to remain patient. Don't expect fast results. From my experience, once it starts rolling for you, your business will scale-up like crazy.

We looked at the different mistakes that you need to avoid with your online business. It is important to steer clear to have a smooth sailing journey.

We had a look at the different people who have made it big using their online business, and you must use their stories as inspirations to fuel your online business.

Chapter 7:

Drop-Shipping in a Nutshell

If you have noticed, huge Amazon sellers always feature more than 100 items on their websites, have you ever wondered why? Perhaps, you have been thinking about how and where these marketers get their products and can sell them at very affordable price. How much do you think that they make in such business deals? Nevertheless, these top sellers get their bulk products through a business retailing strategy called **drop-shipping.**

The essence of Drop-shipping

Drop shipping is a particular type of retailing technique that empowers the retailer to keep no product or item in stock but rather transfers the role of maintaining product and fulfilling customer orders to a wholesaler or distributor. The retailer typically makes his or her money from the difference in retail and wholesale price of the product. On the other hand, the wholesaler or distributor makes money by having a seller that can sell product quickly.

So, anyone can get started with drop shipping and make money from it no matter your status in the society. There are no government rules against drop shippers when once you are doing it in a legal way and you do not need an exclusive license to start listing wholesale items on your website or an auction site such as eBay.

Positive Things About Drop-shipping

There are two significant advantages of drop shipping, and they are as follow:

• You do not need to get a place to hold inventory or even fill your house with products that may get stolen or damaged in the process.

• You do not have to ship anything; your wholesaler shoulders the responsibility to send sold-out products or items saving you time and cost of going to post office as well as problems associated with the weighing of products.

Negative Things About Drop-shipping

You have little control over the product that has been shipped out.

You are going to have difficult describing to the customers the nature and kind of what you have ship especially if you are required to give more information concerning that particular product.

You have little control over the shipment. Supposing the product so shipped gets a loss or damaged along the way or in transit, it is your duty to work with your wholesaler or distributor to rectify the issue or face negative review.

In my opinion, the best way to start drop-shipping is to use Shopify. They ask for a monthly payment, but you don't need to make your own website from scratch – they will do it for you, all you have to do is to list your products and promote it to your customers. From my experience, most profitable is to find a good manufacturer that is willing to ship your products to your clients.

There are many places where you can find products: most popular are Alibaba.com and Aliexpress.com. I suggest you start from these two.

Do Your Research

Research to find a section or category you want to sell in and make notes of how much each item sells for. For example, if any product you wish to sell is selling on $15 at an average price and the price for you is below $5, it's a good margin, but you can always find profitable products.

List your *products*

You are free to list any amount of product with no upfront fees on Amazon. So, getting a professional account for the price of $40 a month so you can lower your selling costs is not a bad idea. Just sign up with Amazon advertising which will get you a free $100 Adwords voucher for promoting your product for free.

Crucial Tip: Look for better, cheap and efficient ways to improve your product. You can discontinue any method that is less efficient and continues with the more efficient one.

Have an Excellent Customer Service

It is your duty to offer the best customer service to your prospective clients and then go extra miles further to meet their needs, but do not go overboard. Make use of quickest shipping available to start your drop shipping business and add handwritten notes as well.

Crucial Tip: Ask for customer reviews after they buy your products. Ask even if it makes you sound too aggressive.

Keep track of Stock

As a matter of importance, you should be aware the levels of your inventory. Your sales might increase when you are low on inventory. Keep track of how many units you have or how many units your manufacturer/wholesaler/retailer have.

Drop-Shipping from Retailer

So once you get the cost from the retailer but just ensure you will be profitable after fees. You can use an Amazon calculator, just search for it on google. Important note: not every retailer will be willing to do dropshipping for you.

Request Money often

If you are on a tight budget to cover the cost of your orders, you can apply for a cash offer straight to your bank account daily from Amazon. After you get this money lodged into your bank account, then go online and make an order for your customers' product from the lowest priced retailer.

Switch to Fulfillment By Amazon Program (FBA)

Sometimes it's more profitable to use Amazon FBA. Switch to FBA only if it makes sense to do so for your product otherwise you are just busy making more money for Amazon.

Section 2:

Throughout this book, it will pair each of the common steps in product development with a similar acceleration tool that will make each step more cost efficient, less time consuming and most importantly more effective. Nowadays, technology allows us to be accessed worldwide, to work anywhere in the World. Your marketing and promotions can reach millions of people. Before, businesses were limited to geography and availability of experts were also very limited.

Best practices in the e-business include value proposition, offshoring, contracting, website optimizing and more. Each of these services has unique comparative tables and are provided to give you a better understanding in deciding which option to use.

This book begins with a discussion of the product development cycle. It will introduce to you new trends and concepts in the main phases of the development cycle. The various online platforms that will help you to augment these trends through automation and delegation. These platforms are easy to use and are relatively cheap. Whether you want your startup business or not, this book will provide you with a working knowledge on how to do it. With the potential for automating and delegating your business processes, you will also see the value of being a hands-on proprietor. You should always expand your knowledge and skills.

This book can only go so far as to provide you with the basics and some advanced principles and techniques of product development and the available power tools at your disposal. As soon as you apply the principles in this guide, the experience will take over as your teacher and business mentor. However, when you seem to forget those websites that can help you with outsourcing your advertising projects or you could not remember what SEO of the company stands for, this Kindle Book will always be here to assist you in your business ventures.

Chapter 8:

Consider and Believe

In this chapter you will acquire information about:
- How to be The 21st Century Entrepreneur
- How to Materialize Your idea
- Lifecycle of Your Product

.

The recent economic problems also present the necessity of having more than one source of income. When big employers started declaring bankruptcy and fired many employees, the need for a reliable source of revenue through your own venture is essential. The most secured job is the one you own. Nowadays, it is not a matter of having one or two jobs, but instead having an own business that can generate money is being used as a contributing factor towards financial freedom and security.

In my opinion, entrepreneurship satisfies the desire for profit. Entrepreneurs want for new experiences and adventures. The thrill of doing something new that is outside of their comfort zone is only enhanced by the bonus of profit and the chance to earn money.

The objective of this chapter is to give you a foundation on the basics of product development. It presents the common steps and techniques an entrepreneur must take to turn his idea into reality. If you are a beginner in entrepreneurship, you may want to read thoroughly on the contents of this chapter. If you already have an experience as an entrepreneur, you can browse through the contents and move forward to the next chapter.

How to be The 21st Century Entrepreneur

"Every great dream begins with a dreamer. Always remember, you have within you the strength, the patience, and the passion to reach for the stars to change the world."

Harriet Tubman

The stereotype of an entrepreneur has repeatedly been challenged for the past decades. Due to globalization, the stereotype has been replaced with a new profile of the modern businessman. Before, if someone talked about entrepreneurship, you imagined a picture of a person wearing a suit and a tie, while going to his business in the middle of town. He advertises his business in newspapers or flyers; he pays for overhead expenses such as staff salaries and office utilities and makes enough money for his family.

Today entrepreneurs come from all ages and backgrounds. You don't need anything much to start your own business. You can manage your business at the comforts of your home while wearing casual shirts and jeans. You do not have to spend a single cent to advertise your business. You can be in your office 24/7 without physically being there at all. The power of the internet! I remember when I first started my own online business, it was very hard to

The modern entrepreneurs are very smart; they have accounts on most social media and most online retailers. They are open to change and seek new gadgets and updates in the features. They are multi-taskers while they may have their regular day jobs, they can run their businesses at the same time. Even mothers, who raise their families, students, who are at school, and a group of friends with a shared passion but without time to be together, can manage their businesses at the same time. **They see challenges as opportunities for growth and change and improvement as necessary.**

However, they must share one thing in common, and that is passion. It is the drive that will motivate them to pursue their endeavor while experiencing the ups of profits or the downs of losses. **Passion is crucial** because this is the thing that will get them through the challenges of their business and give them courage in the face of its risks.

How to Materialize Your Idea

Entrepreneurs may be unable to focus all the time. They have so many ideas for a business that they spread their skills and resources too much. Entrepreneurs cannot filter their thoughts. Their obsessive compulsive behavior is the reason of that. They may also choose business ideas that are very much outside their line of expertise and comfort zone. They may also lack the motivation, initiative, and passion to pursue the endeavor. They need a mentor or a coach.

Despite the millions of people, each with an enormous business idea, product and service ideas, there are also millions of cases when they fail to turn their ideas into reality. It makes me sad hearing stories like that. There are many reasons why these situations occur, such as external factors, for example, the economy, the current industry or the saturation of the market. It can also be the presence of healthy almost unbeatable competitions. These competitions are firmly entrenched in the daily lives of your target customers that you can no longer share the market. There can also be a vast amount of supply that the demand for the product or the service may not be enough to make a profit out of it. These are factors that are outside their control, and these entrepreneurs cannot blame themselves for failing to realize their dreams.

On the other hand, when these people with their bright ideas cannot bridge the gap between idea and materialization is because of the lack of skills and guidance of the process. They have in their hands something unique or something that is on an entirely different level compared to similar products or services. However, because of insufficient information, lack of knowledge or the absence of proper guidance, they fail in realizing their dreams. There is one significant difference between these set of internal reasons and the external factors. Internal factors are within the entrepreneur's control and taking control of them may be the key to achieving the success you so much desire.

With all the ideas running in the entrepreneurs mind, it is easy to lose track of their inspirations or become distracted with other thoughts. Do not allow memory failure or distraction to steer you away from realizing your business idea. If you are in the habit of imagining and brainstorming during your idle time, here are the top eight ways to make sure you never miss out on your "eureka" moment:

1. Write or sketch it in a notebook.
2. Share it with a trusted friend and talk it over
3. Have a voice recorder app if you prefer speaking out your idea.
4. Use sticky notes to post your ideas into a wall that can always remind you
5. Download a diary or notepad app in your mobile phone.
6. Use color codes to organize and differentiate one idea from another
7. Put all of your notes in one place instead of scattered around in your area

8. Use your voice answering machine to record your own ideas

Every entrepreneur must be able to predict the potential of their ideas, but there is a difference between simple speculation and an intellectual guess. Mere speculation may involve too many idealistic and fantastic dreams. These fantasies are not grounded on any facts, statistics or business research. These ideas sound great and perfect, but their execution is almost either impossible or unprofitable for you.

Each person has a wealth of creative energies within themselves, all we have to do is to open them. What they have in creativity, they may lack in guidance. It is important to channel all these positive energies into a tool that can focus their thoughts, filter their ideas and soon realize their business dreams.

Lifecycle of Your Product

There are significant work and effort required to transform your idea into reality. However, it is worthwhile to go through the process since this is the make or break situation for your business. It is where you will be able to focus, filter and formulate your idea into a solid plan.

There are generally eight steps in product development, and each stage has their own tools to complete it. In this book I will only talk about the firs step.

1. Generation Using SWOT Analysis

2. Screening Using Forecasts, Trends and Feasibilities

3. Development and Testing Using Prototyping and Contracting Professionals

4. Business Analysis Using Pricing and Profitability

5. Beta and Market Testing Using Mockups and Packaging

6. Manufacture Using Estimation, Logistics and Contingencies

7. Commercialization Using Advertisements and Promotions

8. Review and Refine Using Introductory Pricing, Competition and Forecasting

It is the first stage of the product development lifecycle. You subject your idea into the rigorous test - SWOT. For example, you want to present a new line of fashion accessories. Your target market can be men, women, and adults, and adolescents. You can either find twenty adult women and group them in one batch or make sure that you have each target market represented in one group. Prepare a list of focus questions before the test. Ask questions to them and document their answers and reactions. Make sure you can trace which opinions or comments belong to which demographic.

Strengths, Weaknesses, Opportunities, and Threats or SWOT, are another tool that you can use when you generate your idea. Assess your idea, what are its weaknesses? Opportunities for your product may be an untapped market or a gap in consumer options. Threats can be logistics or legislation that may interrupt your production or delivery.

SWOT worksheet looks like this:

SWOT ANALYSIS

	Helpful to achieving the objective	Harmful to achieving the objective
Internal origin (attributes of the organization)	Strengths	Weaknesses
External origin (attributes of the environment)	Opportunities	Threats

As you go through this process, you now have information that will either allow you to abandon, refine or pursue your idea. That is the reason the first stage is critical, you can make changes even before you start production and use money or other resources. The time you will spend in doing these activities will have significant effects down the road, and it will prove that they are time well spent.

Now that you have input from your preliminary research using SWOT, it is now time to eliminate imperfections and refine the features of your product. Your tools for this step are forecasting and feasibilities. While SWOT will provide you with current information and opinions, the next task should attempt to assess the future of your product. Some questions that you can ask yourself for this step are:

1. How accessible or replicable is your product?

2. What is the status of the manufacturing industry, can it create your product?

3. Will there be future competition for your product?

4. What are the chances for growth in this product?

5. How will the market decrease or increase in the future?

Based on the inputs of your target market and the results of your research, do you require making changes in your idea? Are you willing to make a change? *How far will you compromise your dream to satisfy the market, customers and yourself?*

These are outstanding questions that you have to answer as early as you can. There are things when you overhaul your idea just for the purpose of meeting the demands of the facts and figures, but in the end, you will feel that it is no longer your idea, you might even feel disappointed. The effect is that you lose your motivation or sense of ownership of the notion. The right drive that triggered your entrepreneurship may be gone because of how far you have compromised your vision for future.

Whether you are a beginner or an experienced entrepreneur, there are times when individuals report an instinct or a gut feeling that their idea is right despite the criticisms and findings. Sometimes your perception is wrong and sometimes it is correct. Make sure you can make an informed decision on your product development but do not let it force you to decide on something that will make you unhappy. Remember, there is a thin line between confidence and arrogance, one can genuinely point you towards the right path, and the other may prevent you from making the best possible outcome for you

Opportunities are usually disguised as hard work, so most people don't recognize them.

Ann Lannders

Chapter 9:

Idea of Your Product

Before you start with the prototype, there is a major factor that you have to take into consideration; you must devote your full attention and time into this since there is absolutely no room for error. It doesn't matter how perfect your idea seems, due to the results of your research, refinements, and compromises; you have to validate its originality. It is where intellectual property and patents come into play. It's not only a matter of innovation but also a matter of protection.

Patents are filed with the government to represent your ownership of an idea. It's your legal tool that you can employ to prevent others from making, selling or copying your idea. The same way this patent protects you; it also protects others who may have already developed the same idea that you have. You cannot say that you have already thought of the notion since you were a child and the other person just thought of it a few years ago. The basis of awarding is the first person who files it in the government and proves his ownership of the idea.

Each jurisdiction and country will have their provisions in the awarding of patents. Currently, most countries, including the US or Latvia has a patent office in charge of intellectual property. However, patents, by their nature as being awarded by a government, is only restricted to the particular country that issued it. That means your idea can only be protected in the country where you issued the claim. However, the World Trade Organization is in the process of interconnecting their patent laws and database to create a universal system that protects entrepreneurs and their ideas, regardless of their nationality.

How to Price Your Product or Service properly

Now that you have a practical idea and the cost of your product or service, you can begin analyzing the product regarding monetary figures. It is where profit and profitability come into play.

There is an entire school of thought on pricing. The challenge is finding and choosing pricing principles that are appropriate for you, your product and your market. For example, one pricing principle states that the price of your product must be within the price range of similar products in the market. For example, if most leather bags are within the thirty to fifty dollar range, then your custom made bag must also be within the average. Anything more will discourage your buyers from choosing your product over the other.

On the other hand, there is another pricing principle that states the most expensive your product is, the more chances your customers will choose it. It is because consumers today associate price with value and quality. A low priced product is assumed to have substandard quality of materials, poor craftsmanship, and a cheap product. The opposite is also true. If a product has a high price, it is thought to be made of high-quality materials, accessible and chosen only be the elite few and a better product. This principle states that the more expensive you price the product, the more valuable and highly desired it will appear to the consumers.

You can also target markets to provide you with information on the cost aside from comparing your price with other products. At times, customer feedback is as important as the market trends themselves. You can make your research by searching the Internet for similar products and find the average costs. Incorporate these findings to triangulate and validate your price, your sources are your research, your consumers and the prices of your own market.

If you are a beginner, or you are introducing something untested in the market, it is way better to play it safe by using the average as the basis for your price range. On the contrary, if you have already established yourself in the market and made a name of your own or your brand, then you can take more risks in the pricing of your product.

Whether you chose an average or higher than average pricing scheme, you must add all these figures to determine your profitability. These prices become your revenues and the cost to sell them becomes your expenses.

Determine your profit margin during this stage. Would you want to double your earnings or gradually build on your profit? If there is a significant amount of investment what is your timetable to break-even and claim profits? Another important consideration is the volume you need to sell or the revenue you need to receive based on your target margins. If you can simulate these cash flows and make them as accurate as possible, you can have a better perspective of not only the potential of your product but also additional information on how you can modify the prototype to suit your margins.

For example, say you have an apple pie as a product. The way you can differentiate it from other products in the market is by using organic apples or all natural ingredients. However, the effect will be a higher cost for production. If you insist on the ingredients, you risk lower sales and thus lower profits. However, your product will lose its fundamental difference from other products and may suffer down the road. I have no correct answer here, everything matters.

The importance of this step is to give you an appreciation of the financial side of product development. Remember it is not only, brainstorming, drawing and testing, but you must also give yourself time to sit and do the math. Some entrepreneurs have the knack for numbers and some do not. Having an accountant or a mentor can help you in this step. These professionals can provide you with budgets, income streams, expense items, legal fees and other payments that must be part of your budgeting.

About Packaging

Another essential process in this step is the product packaging. Aside from the actual functions of packaging such as protection of your product, compression and other physical risks to your product, it is the secondary function that is highly valuable. The packaging does not only provide information about your product but also entices customers to consider purchasing your product. It is where you can strategize how to market and present your product in the most stunning way possible and preferably stick out in a line of similar products on a shelf or an online platform. It is where you can communicate to your potential customers your brand, identity, and uniqueness of your products compared to other similar items on the market. Related to packaging is the point of sale display.

Convenience and portion control are also considerations when you develop your product package. Aside from making your product look good through your packaging, it must also provide comfort when you distribute, ship, stack, store, reuse or dispose of. If you have a consumable product, you have to make use of portion control. On what sizes will you make your product? How will they be dispensed? How can the packaging conform to government standards? Every way to maximize a package must be done, for example, most shampoo bottles are shaped to control the amount dispensed per use. It's also shaped so that an average person can grasp it comfortably and without slipping in the shower.

About Manufacturing

This part requires expert inputs. If your product needs to be created from scratch, you will need to send technical specifications to the manufacturers along with a product safety data sheet. These data will be required by the factory that will make your product.It is not only a list of materials that are needed but actual quantities, sizes, weights and other measurements that will be part of the production line. Depending on your manufacturer, the specifications you provide must meet certain standards for them to accept even your product.

In this step, your team of professionals will be of great help to you, specifically an industrial engineer. This professional can help you turn your prototype or mockup into the real deal. His expertise is in the line of integrating the 4Ms for every manufacturing project. He can link together money, manpower, machinery and materials that will result in your product. He can prepare not only the technical documents that you need to submit to your manufacturer but also much more. Depending on his expertise and your need, he can anticipate the process flow for your product, control resources, and design and optimize your product based on your requirements and specification. If you are not an engineer yourself or if you do not have the capacity to take on the more technical side of the manufacturing of your product, these industrial engineers will be of great help to you and you should not go without one.

The heart of this stage is the manufacturers. You will need a network of factories and point persons to turn your idea into the real thing. Aside from that, you will need to gather quotations on the best deal that you can make. They will expect you to provide quantities, detailed descriptions, materials, colors, finishes, dimensions, weight, sizes and other possible specifications. Your creative team can provide these details for you. Your task is to find the factory that can manufacture the products. Use procurement standards to help you choose the best manufacturer for you.

Another tool that you have to take advantage of is logistics. You may have the best product with the best price and best packaging, but if it cannot reach your potential customers or market in a timely and efficient manner, you may lose money, customers, and even your business. Logistics involves a broad range of systems, from material handling, inventory, transportation, storage and warehousing and also security. Disposal and reuse logistics are used to move surplus or waste made by your product. Green logistics are made to consider the impact on the environment and emergency logistics are for critical events such as anticipated delays in the chain.

1. Logistic capability and presence of contingency measures

2. Presence of dedicated account managers

3. References or reviews from other clients and track record

4. Capacity to serve your need

5. Quality, price and timeliness of their work

Aside from price per every item, you also need to take into consideration other charges that your manufacturer may hide from you. Shipping, handling, insurance, commissions and other expenses will be charged to you and often are not included in the price per item. Another consideration is the time. **Can your manufacturer deliver not only quality items but also in a timely manner?** What are the provisions to protect you from failures on their end. Try to get three quotations from different manufacturers to give you better chances of making the right decision.

About The Launch and Promotions

Your campaign must satisfy the needs of a customer before purchase. These are awareness, knowledge, liking, preference, conviction and finally the actual purchase. In this model, a consumer moves from one step to another until he reaches the decision to buy. That can be superficial or a passing memory of your product. Once the consumer has the awareness, he is now ready for more facts and figures, such as price, benefits, comparison to other goods and other knowledge. Your campaign must be able to make your product desirable than other competitors. Once the customer has all of these, he can convince himself to make the decision; the customer will buy from you. From then, he will choose and purchase your product. With these customer needs in mind, before the purchase, you must make sure that your advertising campaign can satisfy these customer expectations.

When you have the product, designed, packaged, priced and delivered, it is now time to launch, advertise and promote it. Marketing your product is your communication tool to persuade and convince your potential customers to become buyers. It is where you put together your brand, slogan, themes, packaging, collaterals, mass media and other promotions into a powerful marketing campaign.

Review Your Product and Refine it.

To promote your product, it's crucial to sell it at an introductory price first. Although, this may mean a small profit margin, you must view it as an investment. You need to get your product sold and into the houses or uses of your customer. It will produce a multiplier effect and a returning customer effect. If your product is truly the best in the market and wins over your competition, then your customers will act as promoters of your product. Word of mouth will happen, and soon your product may even become a new trend. When you prove your product, your customers will return and patronize your business. These effects would not be possible if you started with a high price.

Another significant force of getting your products out is that you can use the sales as a baseline for your forecasting. How many were sold in a week? Which places had the most sales? These are all paramount data that you can collect and use to anticipate your product's life for the future. When you see a steady increase in acceptance of your product, you must modify it and increase its value and also replace the introductory with a more competitive price.

Measure the sales and other product data regarding volume, revenue, and profit. From these, you can have an intelligent guess on how your product will perform in the next quarter and even in the next year. From these predictions, you can make appropriate business decisions, such as product design improvement, re-pricing, and even new product spin-offs. Once you have the need for a spin-off product or an improved product, it will be a new product to design and the entire product development cycle starts again. Or you can totally re-brand your product with the different name and logo. I have personally done this many times, and it turned out successful.

Chapter 10:

Creation of Your Masterpiece

In this chapter you will acquire information about:
- More About Product Development
- About Market Research
- Outsourcing
- Making Your own Brand

The previous chapter was about building the right foundation for your product development. It was meant to introduce you to the basics of manifesting your idea into reality. Now that you have a solid base, you can build on it with advanced and modern tools for product development. In this chapter author will discuss advanced topics in product development, using new trends and best practices and will tell you about acceleration tools, that will help you in your product development and in your business.

More About Product Development

As a salesman, you must be able to differentiate yourself and your product from the rest of your competitors. While other entrepreneurs may follow the same product develop lifecycle, you can make a unique product through value proposition.

When all the goods are made towards customer satisfaction, your product must go beyond satisfaction. Your value proposition must target customer delight. That means that during your product development you must take into account not only giving the bare minimum that all other products in the market are also doing. Your product must also be capable of providing something special and unique that will convince your customers to choose you and your product above all others.

It is where value proposition comes into the scene. A customer value proposition is a total amount that you promise to exchange to your product with your client's money. It is also your statement that says your product is different from your competitors. If your product shares similarities with others in the market, how can you refine to make it stand out?

About Market Research

"You can't just ask customers what they want and then try to give that to them. By the time you get it built, they'll want something new."

Steve Jobs

One of the most successful companies in the world is Apple. As an entrepreneur, the lesson that you can learn from Jobs is that you must able to use market research and prospecting to anticipate the needs and wants of your target customers. When you can forecast the demand, you are in the better or even the first position to supply it.

Another tool that entrepreneurs can use is market research. You must be able to distinguish market research with marketing research. Although it is used interchangeably, experts suggest differentiating between the two. Marketing research is interested in the marketing side of the business, such as the process and systems that you can set up to link yourself with your customers.

On the contrary, market research is all about maintaining your competitiveness through studying the needs, wants, size and behavior of your market. It is where you also differentiate your customers into segments, based on gender, age, economic status, personality, purchasing behavior, interests and other demographic data. It's meant to modify your product into something that will suit the demand of your target demographic.

Prospecting is a term borrowed by entrepreneurs from the mining industry. While miners dig in different locations in the hopes of finding gold, entrepreneurs use exploration to make strategic conversations generate interest and create sales.

Outsourcing

Production offshoring, a particular term used when you relocate your manufacturing to another country, is currently very advantageous in China. There are many reasons why China holds the top rank in the offshoring industry. The apparent reason is the cost, labor, production and logistics are significantly cheaper in China than anywhere else. Another reason is that the offshoring industry is already set up. The country had decades of experience in the offshoring industry and reached its peak in 2005 when companies came in droves to China. Factories and professionals are already in China to serve your production needs.

In 2015, China expects to have a 25% increase in its offshoring services and entire cities are being built to satisfy the delivery and logistic support needed for the products. In fact 10 to 15 years from now, labor costs are expected to remain favorable to entrepreneurs. Compared to India, Brazil, Philippines, Vietnam and other popular countries for outsourcing, China offers diversification, small risks, and attrition that could harm your product. If you plan to offshore some of your business processes to another country, China is one of the best options.

Traditional manufacturing or sourcing of your products and services were once limited to the locale or geographic boundaries where you belong. Industrial partners were often domestic in nature. As a result of globalization and the interconnection of economies of one country to another, offshoring has become a possible alternative. In offshoring, you can relocate a business process to another country. You can offshore major or a minor process, from manufacturing, packaging, customer service, clerical to even accounting methods. The primary reason behind offshoring is to reduce costs, which in turn increases your profit margin.

Nowadays, the leading countries which received off-shored contracts are China for manufacturing, telecommunications for India and software and graphics development for the rest of the Brazil, Russia along with India and China.

Making Your own Brand

Aside from prototyping and packaging, there is another important concept that you have to apply in your business. Branding takes into consideration not only the tangible elements of your product, such as price, package and the product itself but also the intangible elements. Some of the elements are experience, emotions and association. The goal of branding is to build customer awareness and loyalty to your product through your product's unique identity.

Each brand is different but has the same basic elements:

1, Name

2. Tagline

3. Logo

4. Figures, Shapes & Graphics

5. Colors

6. Sounds, scents, tastes and motion when applicable

When you choose the name, you may choose from many styles. You can use the initials of your company; use words that rhyme, or verbs that evoke desired actions or feelings. You can use your own name or the place where the product originated. You can use fictional names too. For the tagline, use as few words as possible that can represent the product's features or benefits, you can also make it as a call to action to your customers or stimulate feelings and emotions.

Logos and other graphics must have high memory retention and association value. It has reached a degree of awareness that it is often used interchangeably with a photocopy. Remember, there is no balanced formula for branding. What you must do is to make sure that your brand and your employees serve to communicate your product to your potential customers.

Chapter 11:

Acceleration tools

Other great website are:
Upwork and Fiverr!

Use these acceleration tools that are made possible by the Internet and modern technology to help you with the difficult steps in product development. Upwork and fiverr are two of the world's most modern global work platforms that connect individuals from a wide variety of professions to entrepreneurs who require their expertise and experience. These platforms are your power tools that you can use to create a right creative team for your product development. You must not ignore these two power tools if you intend on saving hundreds if not thousands of dollars during your product development process.

These two platforms work similarly by allowing you to interview, review samples and portfolio along with the profile of each professional, called a freelancer. You post your requirement in a description job window. You can categorize it depending on your need whether writing, product designing, software and web development, customer service, business services, administrative support and other professional requirements. You can set a price range and deadline for your offer as well as the specifics of the work you are offering. Here you will be able to find an industrial designer, graphic designer, packaging designers that will contribute to bringing your product to life.

Once you receive proposals from freelancers, you will see their profile, reviews from other clients, the price they will charge and the timeframe they can deliver. You can compare the experiences, prices and other facts about your applicants before making the choice. You can send messages to your applicants through Upwork without revealing your personal emails. Once you have accepted a proposal, your payment will be put in escrow. Take note that the release of funds is entirely within your control. Even if your freelancer already sent through completed work, this will not trigger the release of funds. These platforms will charge freelancers a commission for every payment made.

For example, if you need an industrial engineer, these platforms will be your best alternative to find one. Check their profile, their work experience and another background. Another important part of their profiles that you need to look at are the reviews that they receive from their clients. These platforms make use of a 5-star rating system, the more stars, the better the reviews. Look also at their portfolio; is their design aesthetic similar to what you have in mind for your product? Upwork and Fiverr make it possible for contractors, who are living abroad, to still receive gainful employment. Although they may be geographically separate from you, you can still access their experience and expertise.

Take note aside from a fixed price, you can offer them an hourly rate. These platforms will provide you with tools to monitor their actual work hours so you will only pay them for the time they worked on your project. However, it is still best to choose a fixed price contract.

Make sure you agree on the cost to save you from a headache down the road. That will prevent disputes on payment. To protect you, Upwork has a feature called milestones that will allow you to send payment in batches based on the completed work. Since the release of payment is entirely within your control, you can dispute work quality, timeliness and communication with the platforms' support team to protect you just in case you encounter problems with your freelancer.

Various Advertising Techniques

You have several options that you can choose from for your advertising needs, they can range from the usual to the creative, from the free to the inexpensive and from the traditional to the modern. Free does not necessarily mean no money spent but it can also mean you can do it yourself. Here are some of them:

Free:

1.   Word of mouth
2.   Posting on different forums
3.   Press releases
4.   Facebook/Twitter
5.   Blogs
6.   Samples
7.   Google place
8.   Yellow pages (Online)
9.   Ad swaps
10.   Volunteer for ad space

Nothing beats testimonials from satisfied customers to advertise your products. Never underestimate the power of clients to refer your product to their friends or colleagues. You can add incentive to this word of mouth option by giving a discount for every successful referral.

You can write short articles and distribute them to your local press. They are always looking for new products to feature in their lifestyle section.

If you visit a forum or a blog that is all about the product or service you are selling, you can post links to your site or the address of your store. Members of the forum or followers of the blog will be able to click on that link and see that address on their next visit. As powerful as word of mouth is, social media has a wider reach. Post your product and tag and share as many times and as often as you can.

Samples are another way of free advertisement, go to strategic places to give away your samples. Some websites allow you to swap ads, you post an ad on their site, but you have to post their ad on yours. Another free way to get ad space is to volunteer for local organizations or causes. You can negotiate for a spot in their newsletter or on their next meeting.

Low Cost:

1. Google ads
2. Local directories and community sites
3. Flyers and brochures
4. Various discount coupons

For low cost paid ads, you can always rely on both print and web-based media. Google ads can charge you for as low as $10 a day to attract customers both locally and globally. The best thing about Google ads is you only pay for every click. The traditional advertising tools cost varies but can be more expensive than their online counterparts. Aside from that, they also do not have the same reach as web-based advertisements. Discount coupons have a double effect both as an advertising tool and a sales tool.

Facebook with its billions of registered users is the most effective and suitable way to promote your product or service. The service that Facebook provides is free, easy for you to use. It allows you the maximum benefit of an online advertisement, text, pictures, videos, location, contact details, reviews, and feedbacks. It has both computer and mobile applications making it accessible in and outside the home.

Facebook has finally opened its platform for advertising. It allows for finely tuned targeting based on the profiles of its users. It's where the benefit of utilizing paid advertising in Facebook can be found, and this is what makes it different from traditional media. Not only will it allow you to specify which users will see the advertisement but also on the exact time frame or period. When you have these parameters, Facebook will automatically give you a quoted price for the cost.

There are several options that you can choose from for Facebook advertising. There are adverts, targeting, boosted posts and Facebook offers. Adverts place your ads directly in the News Feed or on the right side panel of every Facebook user. The wider reach you want, the more expensive it will be. The best option is to start with a target audience. In targeting, you can send your Facebook ad depending on a set of parameters. It can be based on location, demographic, connection, purchasing behaviors and interests. For example, your product is an innovated kitchen utensil; you can target users who are mothers, with cooking interests and have bought similar items in Facebook. If you already have an online store, you can choose a boosted posts package. When you post your website link on your page, you can make it appear not only on your page or your friend's page but also on other news feeds too. Finally, Facebook Offers create a virtual coupon that they can bring to your shop or use in your online store discount screen. The good thing about this feature is that the coupons can be shared by users with their friends.

There is no set amount for the price of a Facebook advertisement. Instead, the rates are governed by an ever-changing system based on the advertising needs fellow entrepreneurs like you. For example, the more advertisers are targeting this particular demographic that you also want to target, the more expensive it will be. Facebook has two models that you can from for your advertising needs, CPM or cost per thousand impression and CPC or cost per click. In CPM, you pay when 1,000 people have seen your advertisement. In CPC, you pay when someone clicks your advertisements. Although these are the factors to consider, on the average, each advertisement ranges from $.05 to $5 per click.

Facebook may have varying rates in advertisements, but it will provide you with an estimated cost based on the parameters that you will set. Regardless of the cost, comparative studies show that Facebook is still the cheapest in advertising.

Chapter 12:

Managing Everything

In this chapter you will acquire information about:
- Do The Most Important Tasks Yourself
- Networking

Do The Most Important Tasks Yourself

With all the acceleration tools at your disposal, it may seem that your business can already run itself. You can already offshore or outsource significant or minor tasks, you can automate certain processes, and you can have freelancers do other business-related activities for you. However, as an entrepreneur, especially in a start-up business, you need to discern when to do it yourself and when to delegate.

The reason it is still important to personally do the tasks goes beyond cost savings. Aside from the financial rewards, running your businesses at the early stages provides you:

1. Education and experience
2. Responsibility and accountability
3. Direction and immediate resolution

The best teacher in the entrepreneurial world is an experience. You can enroll in several business management classes but seeing it up close and experiencing it firsthand can provide you with more education and learning. Whether you are a beginner or experienced entrepreneur, a new business with its new product or service, will have its unique characteristics and demand. Even if you have similar activities, chances are, this start-up business will have its own personality.

For example, you may hand over the creation of the online logo to a freelancer, but you cannot just give instructions and think that you are done with your task. If it is your first time, take the opportunity to be involved in the process. Try out the software yourself; make sketches even on a piece of paper or try to revise it on your own when your freelancer has submitted the work. The more you learn about the process, the more independent you can become.

As the owner, you have the command responsibility of the entire business. That means regardless of what happens in the business, whether it was you or a member of your staff who committed a mistake, you are still responsible. Although your employees, contractor or freelancers are accountable for their own work, you alone are responsible for all their efforts. The same way all profits and successes of your business are credited to you so are the losses and failures. As early as possible, you have to take complete ownership of the company, and whether there is praise or blame, you alone have to carry it. You have not only a financial but also a personal investment in the business. While your team may only run the company for the salary, you have a personal stake in the enterprise. In the business, you alone may have the motivation to make the company the best that it can be.

When you are starting a business, not only are the products and the office furnishing and supplies new, the business processes and systems themselves are new and untested. It means that as much as you have planned for the running of the company, there are bound to be errors or mistakes along the way. In a start-up business, the longer it takes for a problem to resolve, the greater its impact on the enterprise.

There is no universal set of rules that you can rely on for running your business; it requires your personal touch and attention. The more you immerse yourself in the day-to-day running of the enterprise, the more you learn and the better you are prepared for its future.

Networking

Networking may be the least of your concern in the start-up business, but it is one of the most important tasks that you have to do when you have settled in on your brick and mortar or online store. Your business may be small at first, but it can grow provided you can get the word out and partner yourself with new contacts.

Aside from online networking, you can also do real life networking. It adds a personal touch to your business and gives the feeling of importance to your contacts.

Networking is not a sales call but an opportunity to generate interest in your business. As much as possible do not attempt to sell your products, you are there for the connections.

Do not try to talk to everyone in your list of contacts instead focus on particular people that have the best chances of bringing in business.

Show genuine interest not only in the potential for business but also for the person. Keep the conversation friendly and build trust and rapport.

Once you have an idea of the profile of your contacts, follow up after 2 or 3 days.

Chapter 13:

Conclusion

Product development can be a long and challenging task for any entrepreneur. Fortunately, the technology of today makes the process more manageable for even novice entrepreneurs. Bridging the gap between your idea and its materialization is made even more possible as long as you are guided by the process flow of product development.

Of course, you cannot do everything by yourself and with a limited budget, you may seek cost-efficient alternatives to hiring employees that can do the work for you. The various platforms on the Internet can provide you with a huge network of professionals that you may need. Engineers, graphic artists, and IT gurus are all available and accessible. On the other side of the product development cycle, manufacturing can also be more cost effective if you can offshore your production needs. Again, you do not have to go to the other side of the globe to look for factories that can serve your need.

When you have your business already set up, whether it is a brick or mortar or an online store, you can rely again on technology to advertise and promote your business. At a significantly lower price compared to traditional marketing, you can reach millions of potential customers through the online ads and links. Several social media are often free to use that can provide the ad space that you need.

Although you can automate and delegate most of the business processes, there is still value in getting your hands dirty and doing the work yourself. You can benefit from firsthand experience through education, negotiation, and networking.

Entrepreneurship and technology have allowed start up businesses to start and succeed. Take advantage of this whole new e-commerce industry and make your idea come true and claim your profits in your own business.

About The Author

Robert Daudish is an author, entrepreneur, composer, fitness enthusiast, energy healer and a lightworker. He studied magick and occultism at the young age under his mentor.

Robert has a passion for living life to the fullest and fulfilling his potential as a human being. At the same time helping others to go beyond their limits and get the most out of this lifetime.

He suggests everyone read the books from following authors - Manly. P. Hall, H.Blavatsky, J. Krishnamurti, Eliphas Levi, Michael Tellinger, Scott Cunningham and many others.

"Do what thou wilt shall be the whole of the Law. Love is the law, love under will."

Love And Light,
Ex Tenebris In Lucem

Resources

These are a few that I recommend, believe me, you won't regret reading any of these books.

Change Your Thoughts – Change Your Life by Dr. Wayne Dyer

Way of the Peaceful Warrior by Dan Millman

The Power of Now by Eckhart Tolle

The Alchemist by Paulo Coelho

Millionaire Fastlane by Mj DeMarco

10X Rule by Grant Cardone

F.U. Money by Dan Lok

The Motivation Manifesto by Brendon Burchard

Copyright

Disclaimer

www.ingramcontent.com/pod-product-compliance
Lightning Source LLC
Chambersburg PA
CBHW060412190526
45169CB00002B/868